youth light inc.

© 2009 by YouthLight, Inc. | Chapin, SC 29036

Cover Design and Layout by GraphicSolutions, Inc.
Project Editing by Susan Bowman

ISBN
978-1-59850-065-3

Library of Congress Number
2008943805

10 9 8 7 6 5 4 3 2 1
Printed in the United States

How Grinner Became a Winner

Featuring Six Stories With Grinner, the Flying Squirrel,
Teaching Children Four Powerful Steps to Becoming Winners in School

Robert P. Bowman, Ph.D., and John N. Chanaca, Ed.D.
Illustrations by Walt Lardner

TABLE OF CONTENTS

What is a Winner?

In this book, the term "winner" and "win" denote effort and personal excellence, not something achieved merely through competition. Attitude, motivation, and determination distinguish a true winner. A young person works to become a winner by developing a positive "I can" attitude and by practicing effective success skills. These adventures of Grinner teach children that they all have the ability to be winners and that they can choose to win by doing their personal best.

About the Authors

Robert P. "Bob" Bowman, Ph.D. is widely recognized for his distinctive contributions to the fields of mental health and education with an emphasis on school counseling. He is especially known as a prolific creator of unusual, effective approaches and programs for helping young people. He is also known as a relentless cheerleader for professionals working with chronically troubled youth.

Dr. Bowman has conducted professional seminars, conference keynotes and/or motivational presentations around the world. He as authored or co-authored 24 books and has been interviewed by many national newspapers, magazines and television programs. Dr. Bowman is an Emeritus Professor of Educational Psychology and served on the faculty at The University of South Carolina for more than 20 years. He is currently the president of Youthlight, Inc. and Developmental Resources, Inc.

John N. Chanaca, Ed.D., has spent more than forty years as a counselor and teacher of elementary and middle school students. He is a nationally known speaker on discipline, motivation, and teaching techniques, as well as a parent educator and Christian marriage and family counselor. In addition, he holds a third- degree black belt in Tang Soo Do martial arts.

Dr. Chanaca was honored by the Christa McAuliffe Fellowship Program and the National Exemplary Small School Program for his work with elementary students in developing and implementing the "Super Student Program"—forerunner to Peer Pals, and "Becoming a Winner." Because of his work, his was awarded a Fulbright scholarship to Japan. This along with his love of the martial arts and work as a Christian counselor provides the basis for his creative works. He is currently a counselor for the Horry County Schools, in South Carolina. Also, John is a board certified counselor by the NBPTS.

{Story 1}
How Grinner Became a Winner

One spring, in the biggest tree of the forest, there lived a family of

flying squirrels. One of the young flying squirrels was different

from the others. He always seemed to smile.

That's why all the other animals called him Grinner.

One day, the young squirrels were ready to fly for the first time.
Grinner's brother and sister took turns as they each leaped from the tree.

You see, flying squirrels don't fly like birds. They just spread out their
paws to open their furry side flaps.
Then they glide to other trees, or to the ground.

Grinner was afraid, but when it was his turn, he leaped too.

But as Grinner started to glide, there was trouble. A sudden wind hit him.
Grinner lost control and began to tumble through the air until…

. . . "ZONK!"

Grinner hit a tree and fell to the ground, landing on his head.

Grinner cried and cried. For weeks, he would not try flying again.

He was sure he would never be like the other flying squirrels.

Grinner kept saying, "I can't do it! I can't! I can't!

"I CAN'T !"

© Youthlight, Inc.

The other animals became worried about Grinner.

"Why don't you grin anymore?" the rabbit asked.

Grinner said sadly, "Because I can't glide like other flying squirrels.
I can't! I can't! I can't!"

Grinner became angry. He stomped his foot on the ground.
Then he ran away into the forest. As he ran, the other animals
could hear him cry, "I'm just a loser!"

Soon Grinner came upon Blackbelt. She was a raccoon who was a karate expert and very wise.

"Hi, Grinner," said Blackbelt. "You look upset. What's wrong?"

Grinner answered sadly, "I'm a flying squirrel, but I can't glide like the others. I feel like a loser." Grinner started to cry again.

Blackbelt listened carefully as Grinner told her all about his feelings. She wanted Grinner to know she understood.

Then Blackbelt said, "Grinner, if you want me to, I can teach you four steps to follow that will help you be a winner."

Grinner thought about this. He thought some more. Slowly, he wiped away his tears. Then he said softly, "Okay."

Blackbelt said, "First, Grinner, you have to believe deep inside of yourself that you can be a winner if you want to. Say, 'I can *be* a winner.'"
And Grinner said it.

"Second," continued Blackbelt, "you must do things that will show others that you are a winner. Say, 'I can *show* I'm a winner,'" And Grinner said it.

"Third," Blackbelt went on to say, "when you have something you need to do, you have to take the first leap to be a winner. Say, 'I can *start* like a winner.'"
And Grinner said it.

"Fourth, always finish with your best effort. Say, 'I can *finish* like a winner.'"
And Grinner said that too.

© Youthlight, Inc.

Then, Blackbelt tied a special white band around Grinner's paw and said, "This white wrist band will remind you of the four steps to becoming a winner."

"I can *be* a winner.

I can *show* I'm a winner.

I can *start* like a winner.

I can *finish* like a winner."

Grinner climbed up the big tree again. Very carefully, he crawled to the edge of the top branch.

At first, he looked down at the ground far below and became afraid. "No way!" he said with a slow shake of his head.

But then Grinner looked at his wristband. He remembered the four steps. So he took a deep breath and shouted, "I can *be* a winner!"

Grinner looked down at the treetops and began to grin. Then he shouted, "I can *show* I'm a winner!"

Grinner lifted his head up, stuck out his front paws, and spread his furry side flaps.

He yelled even louder, "I can *start* like a winner!"

Grinner looked carefully where he was going. Then he leaped from the tree, out and away!

The wind blew Grinner around and he almost hit some trees. But he shouted, "I can *finish* like a winner!" and he looked for a patch of grass where he could land.

As Grinner landed, he tumbled around like a fuzzy little ball bouncing and rolling on the ground.

Then Grinner stood straight up and lifted his little front paws toward the sky.
He grinned the biggest grin any flying squirrel had ever grinned.
And he shouted, "ALL RIGHT!"

Blackbelt and the other animals had been watching. They ran to where
Grinner had landed so they could tell him how proud they were of him.
But they looked all over and couldn't find him. Where was Grinner?

Suddenly, Blackbelt pointed up at the big tree. Everyone's eyes looked upward. And there was Grinner, climbing back up the tree as fast as he could go!

Again, Grinner leaped from the top branch. Gliding seemed to be a little easier this time.

Blackbelt and the other animals were so happy to see their friend grinning and gliding, gliding, and grinning.
And as Grinner flew over, what do you think they heard him shouting?

He was shouting, "I'M A WINNER! I'M A WINNER!"

And that's how Grinner became a winner.

{Story 2}
Grinner Learns That He Can Be a Winner

During the summer, Grinner practiced and practiced flying. Soon, he even started learning some tricks. Grinner was so proud, he decided to try the most difficult stunt he had ever heard of—four flips while diving toward the ground.

To do this trick, Grinner needed to climb to the very top of the highest tree. As he leaped, he yelled, "I'm a winner!" Then he dove. He began to drop faster and faster.

Soon Grinner was falling so fast that the wind pulled and stretched his face until his grin almost reached the back of his head. In a moment, he knew he was ready. He rolled into a fuzzy ball, and began turning his first flip…then a second flip…then a third flip. Suddenly, Grinner felt very dizzy. And right in the middle of his fourth flip, can you guess what happened?

CRASH!

That's right. Grinner crashed into the ground. Several of the forest animals rushed over to see if he was all right. They were relieved to see that Grinner hadn't been hurt on the outside at all. But on the inside, Grinner felt very embarrassed and disappointed.

The other animals tried to help Grinner feel better. But he had lost his cute little grin, and nothing seemed to bring it back.

© Youthlight, Inc.

The next day, Grinner walked slowly through the forest to where Blackbelt lived. She was practicing karate while balancing on a narrow log in the stream.

"Hi, Blackbelt," said Grinner sadly.

"Hello Grinner," she replied. "I heard what happened yesterday." Blackbelt went on in a kind voice, "How are you feeling?"

"I'm still very sad about what happened," Grinner explained. "I've lost my winning feeling, and I can't figure out how to get it back. Can you help me be a winner again, Blackbelt?"

Blackbelt looked thoughtfully at Grinner and answered, "Grinner, you are being too hard on yourself. I know you feel upset because of what happened, but all winners make mistakes sometimes. You have always been a winner, and you still are."

Staring at the ground, Grinner moaned, "But I can't feel like a winner again when I'm so afraid to fly."

Blackbelt thought for a moment. Then she said, "Grinner, you keep saying, 'I can't.' That's the first thing you need to work on. Follow me—I have something to show you."

Grinner followed Blackbelt to her home in the hollow tree.

© Youthlight, Inc.

Blackbelt went inside her home and came out with a strange-looking can. It was covered with pictures of eyes.

Grinner laughed, "That's the funniest-looking can I've ever seen!"

"Yes," Blackbelt said, "It's an 'I Can' can. A very special, 'Things I Can Do Well' can. This 'I Can' will help you think of things you can do well."

Looking puzzled, Grinner said, "I don't understand how this can will help me feel like a winner again."

Blackbelt handed Grinner some pieces of paper and a pencil and asked him to write down some things he could do well.

Grinner thought awhile and then wrote. When he was finished, he read aloud what he'd written. "I can climb big trees to the very top. I can work hard and do a good job with my schoolwork. I can jump over a big rock.
I can be a good friend."

Blackbelt put all Grinner's pieces of paper into the "I can."
She explained, "You see, Grinner, you can do lots of things well. If you thought long enough about it, you could probably fill up this whole can."

"Whenever you have problems," Blackbelt continued, "don't say, 'I can't do it' and give up. Say to yourself, 'I can!'"

"I know!" Grinner said, becoming excited. "Like when I have problems flying and feel down about myself, I *can* remember that I am still a winner."

"Yes—that's it," Blackbelt said. "Remember this 'I Can' whenever you are feeling down about yourself." Then Blackbelt smiled and asked Grinner to sick out his paw with the white wristband. Proudly she said to him, "Grinner, you have now earned the next level of wrist band." She took off his white band and fastened an orange wristband around Grinner's paw.

What a surprise for Grinner! He was very excited. He thanked Blackbelt for the valuable lesson. Then he ran and leaped through the forest shouting, "I can!……. I can!…….I can be a winner!"

{Story 3}
Grinner Learns How to *Show* He's a Winner

It was a bright, colorful fall day in the forest. This was the first report-card day of the year, and many of the animals were running home to show off their good grades to their families. But there was one little animal walking far behind the others looking very sad. Who do you think that was?

That's right, it was Grinner.

You see, Grinner had been so busy flying and playing that he had not worked very hard at his schoolwork. He was very disappointed with the grades on his report card.

Grinner kicked the leaves on the ground as he slowly walked home, dragging his report card behind him. Wishing he had a special friend to talk to, he decided to stop by to see if Blackbelt was home.

Blackbelt was busy cleaning her home in the hollow tree. She was happy to see Grinner and took a break from her work to find out what he wanted.

She spoke to Grinner with a caring voice. "You look upset about something, Grinner."

"I am," mumbled Grinner as he kicked some leaves into the air.

"What's wrong?" asked Blackbelt.

Grinner just stared at the ground holding the report card behind his back.

"What are you holding behind your back?" asked Blackbelt.

Grinner slowly handed his report card to Blackbelt. When she saw Grinner's grades, she understood why he was so sad. Grinner explained, "I tried very hard to do my best in school. I kept saying to myself, 'I can be a winner.' But my report card doesn't show that I am a winner. I just don't understand!"

Blackbelt asked, "Did you ask your teacher what happened?"

"Yeah," Grinner said unhappily. "She said it's my attitude."

"Your attitude! Hmmm." Blackbelt thought for a moment. Then she said, "Maybe I can help. Let's pretend that I am your teacher and we are in your classroom. Okay?"

"Okay?" Grinner replied.

Blackbelt began, "Okay class, we are going to learn the three steps in how to gather acorns." While Blackbelt was talking about the steps, Grinner noticed a butterfly fluttering by. Blackbelt watched Grinner carefully and continued talking about the three steps. Soon, Grinner noticed a caterpillar crawling around on a branch. He picked up the caterpillar, put it on his paw, and began playing with it. Suddenly, he noticed that Blackbelt had stopped talking and was staring at him. Grinner asked, "What did you say, Blackbelt? I didn't hear you."

Blackbelt sat down next to Grinner. "I think I know what your teacher was talking about, Grinner," she said. "It's not enough just to know you are a winner. You also have to show you are a winner. While I was pretending to be your teacher, you didn't show me you where paying very much attention to what I was saying."

Blackbelt continued, "Being a winner means first believing you can be a winner—but it doesn't stop there. You must also show you are a winner."

"But how do I show I am a winner?" asked Grinner.

Blackbelt replied, "With good body language."

"Body language?" thought Grinner to himself. This was a new idea for Grinner. He asked Blackbelt what it meant.

Blackbelt said, "'Body language' is how you say things to others with your body. When you yawn, your face says you are tired or bored. When you sit up in your seat and look at the teacher, your body says that you are listening. That's what 'body language' means, Grinner. Now do you understand?"

"I think so," Grinner replied.

"Right now," Blackbelt went on, "your body language shows that you are listening very carefully to me. Your eyes are looking at me, your face is turned toward me, your arms are still, and you are sitting up straight."

Grinner said excitedly, "I get it! The way I sit and where I look can show my teacher how well I am paying attention. When I have good body language, I will show others that I am a winner!"

"That's right," said Blackbelt with a smile. "You can show that you have a winning attitude through good body language."

"How is my body language now, Blackbelt?" asked Grinner.

Blackbelt looked at Grinner carefully, from head to toe. Now everything about him looked like a winner. "It's terrific!" said Blackbelt proudly. "You have learned this lesson well. Now you know how to *show* you are a winner."

Blackbelt asked Grinner to hold out his paw. Then she said, "Congratulations, Grinner—you have now earned a green belt." Blackbelt fastened a green wristband around Grinner's paw.

"All right!" shouted Grinner as he smiled that famous Grinner smile. As he walked home, Grinner thought of lots of ways he would use body language to show his winning attitude to his teacher.

{Story 4}
Grinner Learns How to Start Like a Winner

The weather was changing. Winter was coming. As he woke up in the morning, Grinner could feel a fresh, cool breeze in the air. His bed felt so warm and soft that he didn't want to get up.

After a while, Grinner's family gathered around his bed and pulled his covers off. They told him it was time for him to get up and start gathering acorns.

This was a very important job. Grinner needed to fill the hole beneath their tree with acorns before winter. His family told him to gather all the nuts under the big oak tree on the hill. These acorns would be the family's only food for the long winter ahead.

All summer long Grinner had had fun flying and playing with his friends. Now he had to work. He complained, "So much work! It's not fair! I'll never get this done. There are so many nuts to collect, I don't know where to start."

Grinner peeked out of the hole in the tree and looked over at the hill where the big oak tree was. It looked very far away. He decided he'd better get started. Slowly, Grinner climbed down the tree and began walking toward the big oak tree. When he finally came to the bottom of the big tree, Grinner said, "Oh no! Look at all the acorns! There must be millions of them!"

© Youthlight, Inc.

Grinner sat down and moaned, "There are so many acorns to gather, I just don't know where to start!"

Grinner began to get mad. He got so mad that he began to stomp on the acorns. Suddenly, from behind the tree, he heard a familiar voice. "Grinner," said the voice, "You just don't know how to start like a winner."

"What . . . ?" asked Grinner with wonder. Then he saw that Blackbelt was standing behind the tree.

Blackbelt stepped out and said, "You just don't know how to *start* like a winner."

"What do you mean?" Grinner asked.

"Well," Blackbelt explained, "when you need to start a job that you don't want to do, don't give up on it or put it off until later. The more you think about all that has to be done, the more you won't want to start on it."

"First," she said, "figure out what you need to do to get off to a good start. Then say to yourself, 'I can start like winner!' Then begin."

"That makes sense," said Grinner. "But how would that work with this job? Look at how many acorns there are to carry back to my nest."

"How many acorns can you carry in your mouth?" Blackbelt asked. "Only about four," answered Grinner.

"Then, to have a good start," Blackbelt told him, "you must begin by carrying four acorns back to your nest. After that, don't stop. Keep coming back to get four more each trip until you are done."

"Hm," said Grinner. "I think I can handle that."

"Then say to yourself that you can start like a winner, and get started right now," Blackbelt said. "Before you know it, your nest will be full."

"Okay, Blackbelt," Grinner replied. "I'll give it a try."

Grinner picked up four of the biggest acorns he could find, stuffed them into his cheeks, and began walking home. He couldn't say out loud "I can start like a winner" because his cheeks were full of acorns. But he said it in his mind over and over again.

A few days later, Grinner ran up to Blackbelt and said excitedly,
"I did it! I filled the nest!"

"I'm so happy to hear that, Grinner," Blackbelt said with a smile.

"Starting was the hardest part!" said Grinner happily. "After that, I just kept
going until I was done. I never gave up!"

Blackbelt said proudly, "That's it! Now you really understand how to start
like a winner." Then she tied a brown wristband around Grinner's paw.
"You've learned another important step in how to be a winner.
You've earned your brown belt."

"Yippeeeee!" Grinner yelled with excitement as he jumped up in the air.
"Yippeeeee!"

© Youthlight, Inc.

{Story 5}
Grinner Learns How to *Finish* Like a Winner

Grinner had learned a lot about being a winner. Blackbelt had helped him a lot during this past year.

Now it was spring. Today, Grinner was in charge of cleaning the nest. It had to be done! The family could barely fit in the nest, because of all of the mess! Neatness counted.

Grinner looked around and said, "This job's no problem. I'll use the three steps to be a winner. First, I'll tell myself I can *be* a winner. Second, I'll use good body language to *show* I'm a winner. Third, I'll take my first steps to *start* like a winner."

Soon Grinner started to toss all the acorn shells, dead twigs, and old leaves out of the nest. After a while, the nest was clean. And there was a big pile of twigs, shells and leaves on the ground beside the tree.

"There, I'm done," said Grinner with a sigh of relief. "The nest is all clean now."

Grinner climbed down the tree, jumped over the pile, and ran off to play in the forest.

Later that day, Grinner met Blackbelt, who was fishing in the stream. "Guess what I did today?" Grinner said to her.

"What?" Blackbelt asked as she scooped up a small fish from the stream.

"I used everything you taught me about being a winner," said Grinner proudly.

"Great!" said Blackbelt. "And did you *finish* like a winner?"

"What do you mean?" asked Grinner, puzzled.

Blackbelt answered, "Once you start a job, it is also important to be sure you *finish* like a winner. Let's go see if you did."

Together, they walked to where Grinner lived. When Blackbelt saw the pile at the bottom of the tree, she looked worried. "Oh dear," Blackbelt said. "You didn't really finish your job, Grinner. You left a big mess at the bottom of the tree. If squirrel hunters pass by, they may notice it—and they will know that squirrels live in the tree. Neatness counts in any job, but especially in this one."

Grinner felt scared when he heard this. "Oh," he said. "I knew neatness counted inside the nest. But I didn't think about outside. What should I do?"

Suddenly Blackbelt became very still. She sniffed the air.

Then she whispered, "Humans! Maybe squirrel hunters." She thought for a moment and then said, "I will see if I can lead them away from your nest while you get rid of these scraps from the bottom of the tree.

Quickly, Grinner, dig a hole and bury all these leaves and twigs and shells! Remember, neatness counts!"

Blackbelt ran off. Grinner quickly started digging a hole away from the tree. When it was deep enough, he began carrying the tree scraps to the hole. While he did this, Grinner kept saying to himself, "I can finish like a winner." So he did the job as carefully and neatly as he could.

Suddenly Grinner heard some rustling in the bushes. Was it hunters? Grinner's heart pounded, but he made sure the last part of the pile was buried neatly. Then he climbed up to a high branch where he could see what was happening.

For a while, all was quiet. Then something stirred in the bushes again. It scared Grinner so much that he nearly fell.

Then from out of the bushes jumped Blackbelt, smiling a very big smile. "It's all clear now, Grinner," she called. "You can come down. We don't have to worry about those humans."

"Why not?" asked Grinner as he glided down to the ground.

"Because they weren't hunting—they were just out walking in the woods. I gave them a little scare anyway." Blackbelt chuckled.

"What did you do?" asked Grinner, his eyes wide open.

"I ran quickly down a tree right next to them, and I think I scared them a little. They turned around and started walking back in the direction they came from," Blackbelt explained with a grin.

Blackbelt and Grinner laughed together. Then Blackbelt looked around to see where Grinner had buried the pile of tree scraps.

"Where did you put the pile, Grinner?"

Ginner pointed proudly to where he had buried it. Blackbelt was amazed. "Look at that!" she exclaimed. "You did such a fine job! You finished like a true winner. You've earned your red belt."

Grinner looked at his red wristband and felt very proud. He gave Blackbelt a special friendly hug!

© Youthlight, Inc.

{Story 6}
Grinner Learns the Black Belt Secret

Grinner rested on the top branch of the highest tree in the forest.
He was daydreaming about everything that had happened during the year.
Blackbelt had helped him in many ways. He remembered how he had earned
the different wristbands. More important than the belts were the lessons
he had learned bout how to be a winner.

Grinner had learned how to be, show and finish like a winner. He felt a lot
smarter than before. But now that he had learned all four steps to being a
winner, what else was left to learn? He decided to go ask Blackbelt.

Grinner spread his furry side flaps, leaped from the branch, and glided down to the ground.

As Grinner started walking, he heard someone crying. He looked around to see who it was. Behind a big rock he saw Flapper, a young eagle who was one of Grinner's friends.

"Hi, Flapper," Grinner said. "What's wrong?"

Flapper answered sadly, "I'm an eagle and I can't even fly. I've tried and tried, but I just can't do it! Sometimes I feel like such a loser!
I can't fly! I can't! I can't! I CAN'T!"

Flapper began to cry. Grinner listened to Flapper's feelings. He remembered when he had said almost the same thing to Blackbelt. He thought about how Blackbelt had helped him.

Flapper felt glad to have Grinner as his special friend. It felt good to have Grinner listen to him. Grinner offered, "If you want me to, Flapper, I can teach you four steps that will help you be a winner."

Flapper thought about this. He thought some more. Slowly, he wiped away his tears with his wing. Then, he said softly, "All right."

"First, Flapper, " Grinner began, "you have to believe deep inside of yourself that you can be a winner if you want to be. Say, 'I can *be* a winner.'"
And Flapper said it.

"Second," continued Grinner, "you must do things that will show others that you are a winner. Say, 'I can *show* I'm a winner.'" And Flapper said it

"Third," Grinner went on to say. "When you have something you need to do, you have to take the first leap to becoming a winner. Say, 'I can *start* like a winner.'" And Flapper said it.

"Fourth, always finish with your best effort. Say, 'I can *finish* like a winner.'" And Flapper said that, too.

Then, Grinner looked around on the ground until he found a white piece of string. He tied it around Flapper's leg and said, "This white belt will remind you of the four steps to being a winner."

Flapper smiled and said, "Thank you, Grinner! Wow! A white belt—this is great!" Flapper flapped around joyfully. Then he said, "May I ask you a big, big favor?"

"What is it?" asked Grinner.

"Would you be my special friend and teacher? I would like to be a winner like you."

Grinner smiled and answered, "Yes, I will be your special friend and teacher. But you will need to be a good listener and a hard worker. Now, show me how you can begin working at being a winner."

Flapper hopped to the top of the big rock, then walked to the edge. As he walked, he yelled out each of the four steps to becoming a winner. Can you remember what they were?

Then Flapper spread his wings and jumped. Soon, Flapper was soaring through the air singing, "I'm a winner! I'm a winner! I'm a winner!"

All at once, Blackbelt walked out from behind a nearby bush.
"Hi, Blackbelt," said Grinner delightedly. "I was just on my way to see you."

Blackbelt smiled and shook Grinner's paw. "Congratulations, Grinner. You did it!"

Grinner was surprised. He didn't understand.
"What did I do, Blackbelt?" Grinner asked.

"You showed that you are not only a winner, but you are also willing to help others be winners too. I am very, very proud of you, Grinner! From now on you will be known as 'Grinner the Winner' throughout the forest. You have just earned your blackbelt."

Grinner smiled his biggest smile ever and shouted, "All right! Thank you Blackbelt!"

Blackbelt tied a black wristband around Grinner's paw.

Grinner went off into the forest with his black belt to have many more adventures. Since then, many are said to have seen him from time to time in different forests. So the next time you are in a forest, try to find the biggest tree. If you're very quiet, maybe, just maybe, you will see a little flying squirrel with a black band on its paw, sitting on top of the highest branch. If you see him, shout, "Grinner is a winner!"

The End?